C|

700
.92
24
Gia

Giants of the arts : Ludwig van Beethoven, Charles
Dickens, Vincent van Gogh. -- New York ;
Toronto : M. Cavendish Corp., 1991.
64 p. : ill. -- (Exploring the past II ; v. 3)

Includes bibliographical references (p. 62) and index.
07480954   LC:91016347   ISBN:1854354140 (lib. bdg.)

1. Beethoven, Ludwig van, 1770-1827 - Criticism and
interpretation.  2. Dickens, Charles, 1812-1870 -
Criticism and interpretation.  3. Gogh, Vincent van,
1853-1890 - Criticism and interpretation.  4. Artists -
(SEE NEXT CARD)

# GIANTS OF
# THE ARTS

**Library Edition published 1991**
Published by Marshall Cavendish Corporation
2415 Jerusalem Avenue
North Bellmore, NY 11710

Typeset by Jamesway Graphics
Hanson Close Middleton Manchester
M24 2HD England

Printed in Spain by Gráficas Reunidas, S. A.

LIBRARY OF CONGRESS
Library of Congress Cataloging-in-Publication
Data

*Giants of the arts:* Ludwig van Beethoven,
Charles Dickens, Vincent van
Gogh.—Reference ed.
    p. cm.—(Exploring the past)
    Includes bibliographical references and
index.
    Summary: Traces the lives of three
prominent figures in the world of the arts:
Ludwig van Beethoven, Charles Dickens, and
Vincent van Gogh.
    ISBN 1-85435-414-0
    1. Artists—Europe—Juvenile literature. 2.
Beethoven, Ludwig van, 1770-1827—Criticism
and interpretation—Juvenile literature. 3.
Dickens, Charles, 1812-1870—Criticism and
interpretation—Juvenile literature. 4. Gogh,
Vincent van, 1853-1890—Criticism and
interpretation—Juvenile literature. [1.
Beethoven, Ludwig van, 1770-1827, 2.
Dickens, Charles, 1812-1870. 3. Gogh, Vincent
van, 1853-1890. 4. Composers. 5. Authors,
English. 6. Artists.]
I. Marshall Cavendish Corporation. II Series.
NX633,G53 1991
700′,91′24—dc20                      91-16347
                                          CIP
                                          AC
ISBN 1-85435-411-6 (Set)
ISBN 1-85435-414-0 (Volume 3)

*Giants of the Arts* is number three in Exploring
the Past II series.

Credits: Front cover Malcolm Chandler; page 1
Vincent van Gogh Foundation/van Gogh
Museum, Amsterdam; page 3
Lauros-Giraudon/Museé d'Orsay, Paris

# GIANTS OF
# THE ARTS

**Ludwig van Beethoven**

**Charles Dickens**

**Vincent van Gogh**

Marshall Cavendish Corporation

NEW YORK · TORONTO · LONDON · SYDNEY · SINGAPORE

# STAFF LIST

*Series editor*
## Jenny Mulherin

*Assistant editors*
## Ray Granger
## Neil Harris
## Rick Morris

*Art editor*
## Frank Cawley

*Assistant art editor*
## Sue Downing

*Designer*
## Kevin Humphrey

*Production Controller*
## Inger Faulkner

*Managing editor*
## Maggie Calmels

## Titles in EXPLORING THE PAST Series

# READER'S GUIDE

*Imagine that you owned a time machine, and that you traveled back to the days when your parents were in school. Your hometown and school would look different, while the clothes, music, and magazines that your parents were enjoying might seem odd, perhaps amusing, and certainly "old fashioned" and "out of date". Travel back a few hundred years, and you would be astonished and fascinated by the strange food, homes, even language, of our ancestors.*

*Time machines do not yet exist, but in this book you can explore one of the most important periods of the past through the eyes of three people who made history happen. An introduction sets the scene and highlights the significant themes of the age, while the chronology lists important events and when they happened to help you to understand the background to the period. There is also a glossary to explain words that you may not understand and a list of other books that you may find useful.*

*The past is important to us all, for the world we know was formed by the actions of people who inhabited it before us. So, by understanding history, we can better understand the events of our own times. Perhaps that is why you will find exploring the past so exciting, rewarding and fascinating.*

# CONTENTS

Fotomas

Mary Evans Picture Library

# INTRODUCTION

Throughout history, the work of great artists has been tied up with the societies, and the times, in which they lived. Sometimes, artists have helped to change society, by changing the way men and women think. Sometimes, they have mirrored it, reflecting the views of the people around them. To fully understand any artist, we have to know something of the society around them. To fully understand any society, we have to know something of its artists.

European society in the 18th century was alive with new ideas. People began to question long-held traditional beliefs. They were more inclined to work things out for themselves, and there was a general increase of interest in science. Fewer went to church, especially in Protestant countries such as England.

### The Age of Enlightenment

Educated people tended to reject the societies they lived in, considering them uncivilized. They looked to Ancient Greece and to Rome for their inspiration. This was especially true of buildings and sculptures. It was customary for young aristocrats to go on a Grand Tour of Europe to admire art treasures and visit ancient sites to learn from the ruins. This period was known as the Age of Enlightenment.

At this time the arts were ruled by the Neo-Classical style, a recreation of the styles of Greece and Romè. Order and proportion were the key words of this style. Emotional expression was kept to a minimum. Poetry, drama, music and painting were all subject to strict rules derived from Greek and Roman pieces. Some musicians, such as Bach and Haydn, and painters like Ingres and David, found that these restrictions gave their work extra power, but many others felt they were unable to express themselves fully.

### Rise of the Romantics

Some 18th-century writers and philosophers were inspired by another aspect of ancient civilizations, the democracy and individual freedoms of Athens and the Roman Republic. In France, Charles Montesquieu (1689-175) and Francoise-Marie Voltaire (1694-1778) attacked the absolute rule of the French kings with satire, while Jean-Jacques Rousseau (1712-78), who had some success as a novelist and composer, scandalized French society with his liberal ideas.

Throughout the century, the themes of individualism and freedom came more to the fore, and in the last 25 years exploded into political action, with revolutionary republics set up in the U.S.A. and France, and into a new artistic movement, Romanticism. The essence of Romanticism was mysticism and beauty, rather than logic and proportion. The typical Romantic hero stands alone against a world full of dark forces, natural and man-made.

Romanticism began, perhaps, in Germany, where the philosopher, Immanuel Kant, attacked the ideas of the Enlightenment and argued that all men should be free to

Lauros-Giraudon Musée D'orsay, Paris

8

make their own decisions about their lives. The writers Johann Goethe (1749-1832) and Johann Schiller (1759-1805) took up his ideas in novels and poetry and Romanticism spread quickly across Europe and across most art forms. In England, it influenced a whole school of youthful poets. William Wordsworth (1770-1850) was inspired by the natural beauties of the country around his home in the Lake District. John Keats (1795-1821) wrote much fine lyrical poetry before his tragically early death from tuberculosis. Lord Byron (1788-1824) and Percy Shelley (1792-1822) were more obviously political in their work, while Samuel Coleridge (1772-1834) wrote long, strange fantasies in verse.

France also produced several great Romantic writers, though a little later than those in England. Some were, quite literally, children of the Revolution. Victor Hugo (1802-85) wrote poetry, plays and novels with Romantic themes, while Alexandre Dumas (1802-70) produced dozens of historical romances, rivaling the work of the Scotsman, Sir Walter Scott (1771-1832).

### Romantic Music and Art

In the world of music, Germany produced Ludwig van Beethoven, generally considered, alongside his contemporary Mozart (1756-91), as the greatest of all European composers. The lushness and originality of his music was the essence of the Romantic spirit, which also showed through in use of natural sounds such as bird song in his music, and in the theme of his only opera,

E.T. Archive Courtesy of Dickens House Museum

E.T. Archive

Fidelio, *about a man unjustly imprisoned and rescued by the heroism of his loving wife.*

There were fewer successful Romantic painters. Partly this was a matter of economics. While writers, dramatists and musicians could appeal to a wide audience, painters had to find a single buyer for their paintings. Most relied on a wealthy patron or on a commission – being asked to make a painting for a set fee. Those who could afford paintings tended to be from the more conservative parts of society, people who would view a Romantic as a wild-eyed radical.

### Social Concerns

Romanticism continued to flourish through the first half of the 19th century. However, the world was changing. From its beginnings in Britain in the late 18th century, industrialization was spreading through the great powers of Europe. The invention of the steam engine gave a great boost to heavy industry, and a few industrious people become very wealthy very quickly. The old agricultural order broke down as people flocked from the countryside to find work in the city factories. Social relationships became confused as whole new classes sprang up; factory owners and a large working class.

Increasingly, this new social order became a subject for writers, especially novelists, who found a rich subject matter in the harsh conditions of industrializing countries and the teeming, complex life of the big cities. In England, where the witty novels of Jane Austen (1775-1817) had already chronicled the social life of the countryside, Charles Dickens set about exposing the evils of city life, some of which, such as child labor and the imprisonment of debtors, he had experienced in his own family. Dickens' work was enormously popular, and inspired many reforms.

In France, Honoré de Balzac (1799-1850) described the way ordinary French people dealt with the Revolution and the rule of Napoleon in a series of more than eighty under the general title of La Comédie Humaine, *while Gustave Flaubert (1821-80) wrote of the new middle classes in* Madame Bovary. *In Russia, Nikolai Gogol (1809-52), Feodor Dostoyevsky (1821-81) and Leo Tolstoy (1828-1910) all produced long, complex novels of 19th century life.*

### The Challenge of Technology

Few painters or sculptors rose to the challenge of depicting the new industrial society around them. The English painter, J.M.W. Turner (1775-1851) did paint steam trains, but only as part of his experiments with painting light on clouds and landscapes. England's other great painter of the time, John Constable (1776-1837), though he made many technical advances in the painting of landscapes, always chose as his subjects the timeless rural scenes he had known as a boy in his native Suffolk.

By the 1850s, painting was under threat from a whole new source. A Frenchman, Louis Daguerre, and an Englishman, William Fox Talbot, had independently invented ways of taking photographs in the 1830s. Though their early experiments were very primitive, by 1850 it had become possible to make sharp, detailed images. Photographic equipment was so bulky and complicated that few people were out and about taking pictures, but every small town had its photographic studio, where people could have their photographs taken for a fraction of what they would have to pay even the cheapest portrait painter.

### New Ways of Painting

Photographers boasted that their new cameras would be the death of painting, but they were only half right. What suffered was the sterile, Academy-inspired style of portrait painting.

Photography provided an inspiration to painters to find new ways of depicting the world. In England, a group calling themselves the Pre-Raphaelite, Brotherhood produced colorful, superbly detailed work, with everything in pin-sharp focus, that recalled the styles of the 14th and 15th centuries.

In France, another group, the Impressionists, looked to photography for inspiration. Fascinated by the varying moods of light and shade in photographs, they resolved to take their easels out of the studios and paint directly from nature, attempting, like a photographer, to capture the fleeting moment. Impressionists developed various techniques for bringing scenes to life and experimented with the way the human eye perceives color.

These new techniques were used by Vincent van Gogh not just to record a scene, but to paint the way he felt about what he was looking at. In this, he was one of the most important forerunners of the artistic movements of the 20th century when, confronted with war and devastation on a tremendous scale, artists of all kinds attempted to express their feelings and their own unique vision of the world in their work.

# Ludwig van
# Beethoven

Beethoven's childhood was a poor and unhappy one. His musician father was a drunkard who bullied his son into learning music. Despite this bad start, he moved to Vienna, where his talent developed until he became a celebrated pianist, teacher and composer. He was happy doing this until disaster struck; he began to go deaf while still in his late twenties. This tragedy forced him to concentrate on composing music rather than playing it. Basically a kindly man, Beethoven was much loved by his friends, who tolerated his eccentricities and outbursts of temper.

## Brilliant and rebellious, Beethoven broke the rules of music and manners – but won everlasting popularity.

One cold winter's night, little Ludwig van Beethoven woke up in terror. He could hear a glorious voice singing. Ludwig knew it was his drunken father, Johann. Now he would be dragged out of bed in the freezing attic to have the music lesson he had missed.

The family lived in Bonn, now the capital of Germany, but then just a lovely little town on the River Rhine. Vineyards and orchards spread down to the water, and old castles stood on soaring rocks. The family were very poor. Johann, who worked as a court musician, spent his wages on drink. When Ludwig was born in their wretched attic one freezing day in 1770, Johann decided he must teach him to be a brilliant child musician, like Mozart.

Little Ludwig started learning the clavier (a forerunner of the piano) when only four. He would stand for hours playing, with tears running down his cheeks, tired after school, hungry and dirty. Yet he made up variations on this instrument that were so beautiful, people would stop in the street to listen.

Ludwig also learned the violin and viola. He gave his first concert when he was eight, and left school at the age of ten to perform in Holland. This was not successful, so the next year he started work as a court musician,

## Personal Profile

**LUDWIG VAN BEETHOVEN**
**Born** *December 16, 1770*
**Died** *March 26, 1827*
**Parents** *Johann van Beethoven and Maria Magdalena Keverich*
**Personal Appearance** *A short, thickset man with an unusually large head. As he grew older, his hair became longer and more unkempt. Very expressive face with strong features, a high forehead and gleaming eyes. A generous smile.*
**General** *A passionate, emotional man, dedicated to his music and indifferent to social conventions. Shrewd in business, temperamental in relationships and idealistic in his belief in freedom and justice.*

*Beethoven's grandfather, Ludwig (above), was court musician to the powerful Elector of Cologne. He passed on both his name and his musical gifts to his grandson.*

*The Beethoven family lived in Bonn, Germany (above right), on the River Rhine. The Elector of Cologne had his court there.*

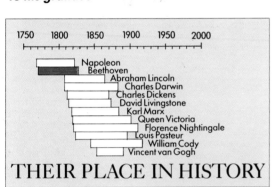

| 1750 | 1800 | 1850 | 1900 | 1950 | 2000 |
|------|------|------|------|------|------|

Napoleon
Beethoven
Abraham Lincoln
Charles Darwin
Charles Dickens
David Livingstone
Karl Marx
Queen Victoria
Florence Nightingale
Louis Pasteur
William Cody
Vincent van Gogh

## THEIR PLACE IN HISTORY

*Beethoven was born on the second floor of this house (above) in Bonn. It is now a museum.*

and when he was only 12, his first compositions were published.

On a magical visit to Vienna at the age of 16, Beethoven played to Mozart, who said, "Keep your eyes on that fellow; one day he'll give the world something to talk about."

Beethoven had to rush home from Vienna, as his beloved mother was dying. There followed five years of hard work as a court musician, while he struggled to manage his drunken father and support and look after his two little brothers. He was always to feel responsible for their welfare.

He moved to Vienna at the end of 1792. In this glittering capital city, he studied with some of the finest composers in the world, including Haydn, Mozart's mentor. They were not on good terms, but Beethoven

*When Beethoven was 16, he visited Vienna for the first time. The highlight of his visit was meeting Mozart, then 31 (right). As he improvised on the piano, Mozart was so impressed that he forecast that Beethoven would astound the world. Beethoven's visit was sadly cut short by his mother's illness.*

*Prince Karl Lichnowsky (above) was one of Beethoven's first patrons. He gave the composer financial security.*

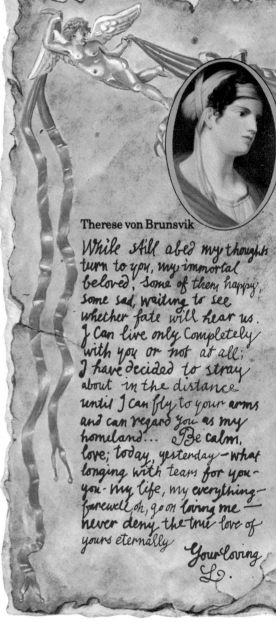

Therese von Brunsvik

*While still abed my thoughts turn to you, my immortal beloved, some of them happy, some sad, waiting to see whether fate will hear us. I can live only completely with you or not at all; I have decided to stray about in the distance until I can fly to your arms and can regard you as my homeland... Be calm, love; today, yesterday — what longing with tears for you — you — my life, my everything — farewell oh, go on loving me — never deny the true love of yours eternally*

*Your loving*

*L.*

gained a superlative training in composing classical music.

Beethoven was also a brilliant keyboard player. He began to give concerts, to teach, and to sell his compositions. The rich, musical Prince Lichnowsky helped him financially and introduced him to other music-loving aristocrats. After such a sad childhood, Beethoven was happy at last, with rich patrons, eager pupils and many friends.

Suddenly however, when he was only 28, Beethoven suffered a terrible tragedy. A strange whistling and roaring began in his ears. As it grew worse, he realized he was going deaf. His career seemed to be in ruins, and he began to feel so ill he expected to die. He went to rest at Heiligenstadt, a village outside Vienna, and from there he wrote a "will" to his brothers, explaining how isolated from other people his deafness made him. He wanted to commit suicide, but felt he should stay alive to write his music.

As his deafness increased with the years, he became shy, sensitive and very quarrelsome. His servants often ran away and his rooms became a mess of papers, old food, dirty clothes and unemptied chamber pots. He composed very slowly, covering the paper with corrections, forgetting to eat and pouring jugs of water over his head to cool off. Once he nearly lost the manuscript of his great Mass in D, because the maid had

**Beethoven moved to Vienna in 1792. He would meet his friends in cafés (above), and took his conversation books with him when his deafness required written, not spoken, words. In 1802, on his doctor's advice, Beethoven spent the summer at Heiligenstadt (below).**

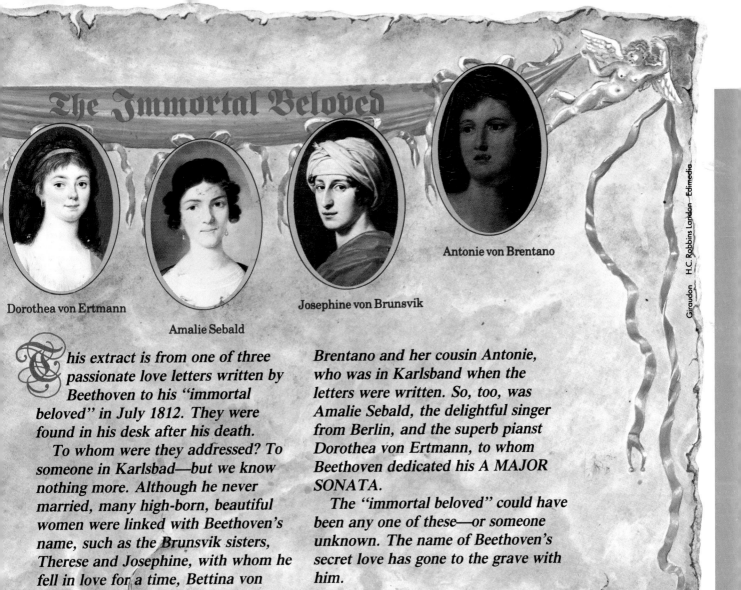

# The Immortal Beloved

**Dorothea von Ertmann**

**Amalie Sebald**

**Josephine von Brunsvik**

**Antonie von Brentano**

This extract is from one of three passionate love letters written by Beethoven to his "immortal beloved" in July 1812. They were found in his desk after his death.

To whom were they addressed? To someone in Karlsbad—but we know nothing more. Although he never married, many high-born, beautiful women were linked with Beethoven's name, such as the Brunsvik sisters, Therese and Josephine, with whom he fell in love for a time, Bettina von Brentano and her cousin Antonie, who was in Karlsband when the letters were written. So, too, was Amalie Sebald, the delightful singer from Berlin, and the superb pianst Dorothea von Ertmann, to whom Beethoven dedicated his A MAJOR SONATA.

The "immortal beloved" could have been any one of these—or someone unknown. The name of Beethoven's secret love has gone to the grave with him.

mistakenly wrapped his boots in it!

Beethoven wrecked his pianos in his efforts to hear his own playing. From 1812, he used ear trumpets, but by 1818 he was completely deaf and had conversation books for people to write in. Orchestras became quite confused by his conducting. At the first performance of his great Ninth Symphony on May 7, 1824, he beat time beside the conductor, Umlauf. When the music came to an end, he went on counting out the beat, until a singer gently turned him to face the tumultuous applause.

Short and heavy, with wild, flying hair, Beethoven began wearing old, torn clothes and was once arrested as a tramp by the police. Despite this, he had a commanding

**Karl, Beethoven's adored nephew (above), was made miserable by his uncle's attempts to keep him from his "wicked" mother.**

appearance; he was also great fun at parties, and extremely kind. His huge circle of friends adored him and put up with his fearsome temper.

Musicians before Beethoven had worked for rich patrons as servants. Beethoven wrote wonderful music for the aristocracy, but accepted their money and friendship as his right. He refused to be told how to behave, even when he was at court. "There are thousands of princes, but only one Beethoven", he wrote. It was a point of view in line with ideas of equality spread by the French Revolution.

In music, too, Beethoven refused to be bound by strict rules. His powerful inspiration gave him the confidence to change the

*Until he became deaf, Beethoven was famous as a brilliant pianist. His deafness caused him to turn to composing – writing down the music he heard in his head. His last compositions were created mainly on this piano in his study (left).*

rules. You can even hear cuckoos and a thunderstorm in his country symphony, the *Pastoral*. After this, other musicians began to compose "romantic" music, freely expressing their feelings. In all, Beethoven wrote symphonies, concertos, sonatas, quartets, songs and one opera, *Fidelio*.

Towards the end of his life, however, he composed little, spending his time on lengthy lawsuits to gain custody of his young nephew, Karl. He won the case, but Karl was miserable, and felt persecuted by his uncle. Later he attempted suicide. It was

*Beehoven's funeral (left) took place in Vienna on March 29, 1827. A huge crowd gathered in front of his last residence, the Schwarzspanierhaus (at the back of the picture, to the right of the church). In 1888, his remains were removed from Währing Cemetery to Zewntral Friedhof, where he lies next to his fellow-composer, Franz Schubert.*

## Personal Effects

*Some of the great composer's most important belongings: his violin, walking stick and a variety of ear trumpets – the latter only of limited use.*

after this shock that Beethoven abandoned his plans for an academic career for Karl, who entered the army.

At this time, too, Beethoven was suffering several illnesses. He died on March 26, 1827, shaking his fist at a thunderstorm. Twenty thousand people came to his funeral.

*An original and unconventional artist, Beethoven's appearance was an easy target for cartoonists (right). Their drawings were humorous, rarely nasty.*

# AUSTRIA v NAPOLEON

**Austria was a courageous and persistent enemy of Napoleon is but nonetheless lost land and power in the final settlement.**

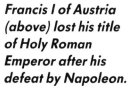

Bridgement Art Library

**Francis I of Austria (above) lost his title of Holy Roman Emperor after his defeat by Napoleon.**

Two hundred years ago, in 1789, Europe was thrown into turmoil by the French Revolution. Austria, like most European states, was afraid of the spread of revolutionary ideas, but was particularly angered by the execution of the French queen, Marie Antoinette, an Austrian princess. Austria proved to be the most persistent of France's enemies, and kept returning to the battle front, even after the most devastating defeats.

Austria, together with Prussia, invaded France, but the French, under their brilliant leader Napoleon Bonaparte, drove them back. The French seized the west bank of the Rhine and marched on into Germany.

At that time, Germany was not the country we know today. It was divided into hundreds of small states and many formed part of the Holy Roman Empire. This had been set up a thousand years before by the mighty king of the Franks, Charlemagne, the first Holy Roman Emperor.

At the time of the French invasion, the

Holy Roman Emperor Francis, who was of the Austrian Hapsburg dynasty, had little power over the other princes. Prussia made peace with France, and Bavaria and several other German states joined Napoleon. By 1801, after a long series of French victories, the Emperor Francis did finally give up. Napoleon reduced the German states to 30 in number, greatly weakening the Holy Roman Empire.

In 1805, Napoleon poised 180,000 French troops on the coast ready to invade Britain,

Giancarlo Costa

***Napoleon in camp at Austerlitz (right), where he routed the Austrian army through his brilliant strategy.***

then allied with Russia, Sweden and Austria. Two great Russian armies were on the march and the allies planned a three-pronged attack with 350,000 troops. The Emperor Francis joined them and marched into Bavaria. Napoleon, abandoning his invasion plans, threw his "Grand Army" across Europe so rapidly that part of the Austrian army was taken by surprise and surrendered.

On November 13, Napoleon's army entered Vienna, which was in a state of shock. The Emperor had fled east to his lands in Moravia, and Napoleon occupied the imperial palace of Schonbrunn. One week later his

officers attended the first performance of *Fidelio*.

All did not go well for Napoleon, however. His fleet had been shattered at Trafalgar. A great Russian army and 80,000 men under the excellent Austrian military leader, Archduke Charles, were approaching. Napoleon decided to lure them into battle near the small town of Austerlitz, and here he smashed the entire Austo-Russian army.

In the settlement afterward, Austria lost much of her land. Napoleon became president of a new organization of German states, called the Confederation of the Rhine. This confederation broke up the Holy Roman Empire

Nick Harris

19

and Francis lost his title, becoming simply Emperor of Austria.

By 1809, Austria had recovered, and in Vienna, every theater, coffee house and dance hall rang with patriotic songs. The Archduke Charles invaded Bavaria on April 9, calling all Germans to rise against Napoleon, but none did. Only the mountain people of the Tyrol responded, under their

*Napoleon united the German states he had conquered to form the new Confederation of the Rhine in 1806 (above). By altering old boundaries, he dismantled the remnants of the Holy Roman Empire.*

*The young Austrian princess, Marie Louise, with the French Emperor, Napoleon I (left), arrive in grand style at the Tuileries Palace in Paris on the day of their wedding. Napoleon hoped that this marriage would strengthen his hold on Europe.*

# VIENNA OCCUPIED

During the Napoleonic Wars, Vienna was occupied twice by the French. In November 1805, the defeated Emperor Francis negotiated for the French to enter the city peacefully. Secure in their victory, they then withdrew, until, in May 1809, the Austrians rose up once more and brought Napoleon's army back to Vienna.

*The French assault on Vienna in 1809 lasted less than 24 hours (above and right). Napoleon himself directed the bombardment which defeated the Austrians. The French swarmed into the city over pontoon bridges.*

peasant leader Andreas Hoffer, who fought a brave guerrilla campaign until he was caught and executed.

Five weeks after the invasion of Bavaria, Napoleon entered Vienna again, this time after a heavy bombardment. Beethoven hid in his brother Karl's cellar, with pillows tied over his ears. Poor Haydn, who was 77, died three weeks later from the shock of the occupation.

Napoleon suffered his first defeat at Aspern-Essling, outmaneuvered by Archduke Charles and the Austrian army. The Austrians did not exploit their success, however, and Napoleon made new plans. On July 4, the French made a daring night crossing of the River Danube during a thunderstorm and completely surprised the Austrian forces, finally defeating them at Wagram. The casualties on both sides were appalling. In the peace terms, Austria lost more territory and had to pay the French compensation.

The clever Austrian Foreign Minister, Metternich, knew that Napoleon desperately needed a royal heir, and he negotiated for Napoleon to divorce his beloved Josephine and marry Emperor Francis's daughter.

They were married in Paris on April Fool's Day, 1810. Soon Marie Louise had a son, the little golden-haired King of Rome.

The tide was turning against Napoleon, however. The British under Wellington were advancing in Spain. Then, in 1812, Napoleon made a disastrous decision to invade Russia, and lost nearly 600,000 troops. The German states turned against Napoleon as he retreated to France. The nations of Europe pursued him and, after many battles, forced Napoleon to abdicate.

With the removal of French rule, the new borders of Germany had to be agreed at the Congress of Vienna, which began in September 1814. Countless sovereigns and heads of state streamed into Vienna and the Emperor played host. The cost was huge – $100,000 a day to feed the guests alone! In addition there were fabulous entertainments: balls, sleigh parties, hunting trips, fireworks' displays and a concert season that opened with Beethoven's *Fidelio*.

The settlement that was finally reached in June 1815 gave back to Austria most of her lost territories. Prussia, however, was put in the position of guarding Germany's western frontier, and the balance of power shifted in her favor. The remaining 39 German states formed a new confederation. The war with Napoleon had destroyed the old political structure of Germany, and, with it, much of Austria's power.

*French troops (below) being drilled in Vienna after their conquest of the city.*

Bildarchiv Preussischer Kulturbesitz

Mauro Pucciarelli

*All the heads of state in Europe met for peace negotiations at the Congress of Vienna in 1814 (left). They hoped to reclaim the old borders of Europe, but this was not achieved in the settlement which took away some of Austria's power.*

*The Austrian Foreign Minister, Metternich (left), was an important signatory to the Treaty of Vienna (right) which gave Europe peace for 40 years after the Napoleonic Wars.*

BPK

# Fidelio.

The soprano Anna Milder (later Hauptmann) tells of her experiences singing in various productions of the opera *Fidelio*.

W hat a night! I'll never forget it. I was only 19 and singing the title role in the very first performance of Beethoven's opera *Leonora*. It was November 20, 1805. Later the opera's name was changed to *Fidelio*. What a pity – I liked *Leonora* better.

Leonora is the real name of the heroine. She rescues her husband Florestan by dressing up as the boy Fidelio ("the faithful one") and going to work in the prison where he is unjustly held. In the dramatic final act, she saves Florestan by threatening the villainous governor.

The opera is based on a French text by J. N. Bouilly. The incident actually took place during the French Revolution, at Tours where Bouilly was an official. To protect himself, Bouilly transferred the setting of the action to Spain. This kind of rescue story was very popular in Europe at the time.

I had to wear trousers, of course! I was rather fat then and I hadn't sung on stage much, so I was terribly nervous. The music was extremely difficult, especially as Herr Beethoven kept changing it all the time.

*Anna Milder-Hauptmann (left), a famous soprano and the first leading lady in* Fidelio. *The 1814 revival is advertised below.*

He would stride about the Theater an der Wien, where we were putting on the opera, shouting at everyone. He threw an ink pot at the first violin and at one point he came up to me, snatched my music from my hands and tore it up. "You will never be my Leonora," he stormed. But when I burst into tears, he put his arm around me and said, "There, there. You are young. In time you will be a great singer." However cross he got, you always forgave him. He was so kind. I am sure it was his deafness that made him get angry.

Beethoven quarreled with the manager of the theater, Baron Peter von Braun. I didn't like him either. He was really a banker, not a theater person. He made Beethoven write with the librettist, Sonnleithner, but the poor writer just wasn't very good at dramatic plots. Beethoven re-wrote and re-wrote, attempting to put the drama into the music because it was so lacking in the text.

Then, one week before the first night, disaster struck. The French army was near Vienna. Many of Beethoven's aristocratic friends fled – and we lost our first-night audience. Then all hell broke loose.

People were looting the shops and there were bread riots. The grenadiers opened fire, and a hundred people were injured or killed.

## FLASH BACK

# The Romantic

The Romantic era began in the 1770s. It was based on ideas of personal freedom and choice, and swept away the cool reason of the preceding Age of Enlightenment. Man saw himself standing alone against a world of conflict, as in "The Wanderer" (right) by the German painter Friedrich.

The German writer Goethe (right) inspired Romantic poets and musicians. In his works, his heroes question their world.

A scene from Faust (below), Goethe's most famous drama.

*Spirit*

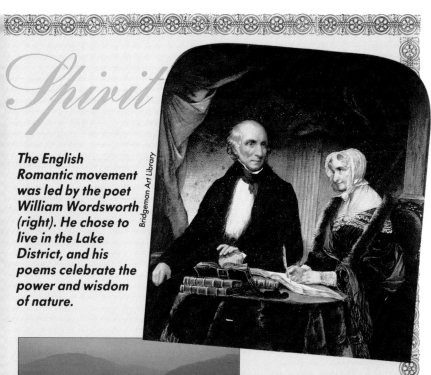

**The English Romantic movement was led by the poet William Wordsworth (right). He chose to live in the Lake District, and his poems celebrate the power and wisdom of nature.**

*Bridgeman Art Library*

**The Romantics believed that nature could mirror human emotions. A lonely misty landscape (left) was seen as a reflection of a solitary, brooding mind.**

*Fotobank/England Scene*

**The Romantics loved all things medieval. A Scottish poet, J. MacPherson, wrote epic poems inspired by Celtic literature. He claimed to have translated them from a Celtic bard, Ossian. These intense, strange tales, of which one scene is shown on the right, inspired Romantic artists and writers throughout Europe, and gave birth to a new style of literature.**

*Fotomas Index*

*E.T. Archive*

Soldiers started to clear the houses in the suburbs. Luckily I lived near the theater, or I don't know what would have happened.

Eventually the Emperor decided to hand over the city peacefully to the French. They marched in, a ramshackle bunch, under their handsome leader, Prince Murat.

The city was as quiet as death. Instead of the usual ceaseless rattle of coaches lumbering through the streets, you scarcely even heard a cart creeping by. If anything moved, the French grabbed it, so everyone stayed at home where they felt safer.

The theaters were empty. We discussed the situation, of course, and it was decided that *Leonora* was just the thing to distract everybody. The show must go on!

It was such an anticlimax. The few people who came were mostly French. Of course, the opera was in German, so they couldn't understand one word. And Beethoven had insisted on writing an entirely new overture, which the orchestra didn't know. Anyway, we were all far too worried by the war to sing our best.

The old composer Haydn came backstage afterwards. "My dear girl," he told me, "you have a voice the size of a house." Unfortunately I heard someone sniggering, "And not just her voice, either." I felt very depressed. The reviews were pretty bad and, after only two more performances, we closed.

Poor Beethoven. His friends dragged him off to his patron Prince Lichnowsky, and insisted on going over the whole opera to work out what was wrong. They decided it needed shortening from three to two acts. According to Rockl, who sang the part of my captive husband Florestan, Beethoven's friends had never seen him in such a fury. From seven o'clock in the evening until one in the morning, arguments raged. At last he agreed to the cuts, a delicious supper was served, and Beethoven was the life and soul of the party.

The new version of *Fidelio* was performed the next spring, but there were more problems. Beethoven's new overture still didn't seem right, and there was too little rehearsal time. Beethoven screamed that his music

# FLASH BACK

# BIEDERMEIER PERIOD

"Biedermeier" was the name given to a plain, uncluttered style of furnishing (right), and reflected German middle-class taste.

*Bayerisches National Museum*

Minimum ruffles were used in clothing (above) and the cup (right) is decorated with a picture of the kind of good solid German citizen who would use it.

*Bayerisches National Museum*

Function, not decoration, was the keynote of the style, as demonstrated in this kitchen (left), and the discreet ornament of the clock (below).

*Archiv für Kunst und Geschichte*

*Christie's Colour Library*

*Macdonald/Aldus Archive*

was being murdered and flew into a violent rage with the manager, Baron von Braun. He accused von Braun of cheating over the profits, demanded his music back and rushed out of the theater.

We didn't perform the opera again for eight years. During that time, I had become famous. It was three actors from the Kärntnertor Theater in Vienna who wanted to revive *Fidelio*. This time the lyrics were written by the wonderful Treitschke.

The great Radichi sang the part of Florestan. We were all tremendously excited. On the first night Beethoven was frantic. He hadn't managed to finish yet another new overture. They had to use one of his old ones – I didn't even hear which one. I was too busy getting into my trousers and putting up my hair.

It was a sensational success. Everybody was in a good mood because the war was over. The new overture, played at the second performance, was a triumph. And when the chorus of wretched prisoners came out of their dungeon and sang their farewell, there was not a dry eye in the house.

# Charles
# **Dickens**

When he was 12 years old, something happened to Charles Dickens that was to haunt him for the rest of his life. He experienced, first hand, the misery of poverty when his father was imprisoned for debt and he was forced into the harsh world of the child factory worker. This personal knowledge enabled him to write so movingly about the poor and the helpless that their plight touched the hearts of millions of readers. In this way Dickens, the most popular novelist of his day, was also a great influence on the social reforms that took place in Victorian England.

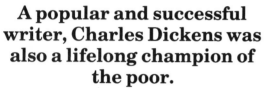

# A popular and successful writer, Charles Dickens was also a lifelong champion of the poor.

ne evening in March 1870, Charles Dickens stood on the platform of St James's Hall in London while over 2000 people cheered and clapped. His cheeks were wet with tears, for he had just completed the last of his famous public readings. Never again would he experience the excitement of performing before a large and captivated audience.

Since 1858 he had been on several public tours of Britain and Ireland, and one of America. As a powerful performer as well as a writer, his appearances were received with great enthusiasm by audiences who knew and loved his novels and appreciated his skill at making them laugh and cry.

Perhaps because Dickens put so much energy into the readings, they took a toll on his health. By 1870, he was in a state of total exhaustion and he retired to the countryside to work on what was to be his last novel.

His writing earned him a reputation as

*Victoria & Albert Museum*

## Personal Profile

**CHARLES DICKENS**
**Born** *February 7, 1812*
**Died** *June 9, 1827*
**Parents** *John Dickens and Elizabeth Barrow*
**Personal Appearance** *Dark, deep-set eyes, a high forehead and full lips. In his early 40s, he grew a mustache and a flowering, curly beard.*
**Personality** *His humor and friendliness assured his great popularity. A man of sincerity and great humanity, he enjoyed his enormous fame without conceit.*
**General** *Even as a child, he was very observant of people and places and retained vivid memories from his earliest years. In his day-to-day life he was very methodical and kept to the same routine wherever he was, yet his creative energy drove him into many diverse activities — traveling, acting, lecturing and writing.*

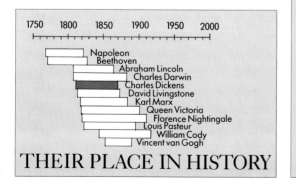

## THEIR PLACE IN HISTORY

*Dickens' father (left) was a clerk in the Navy pay office. He met his wife, Elizabeth (right) through her brother, who was working in the same office.*

entertain his father's friends with comic songs when they came to visit.

This situation was not to last, however, as his father was careless with money and unable to provide for his growing family. He was imprisoned for debt, and Charles, now 12, was sent to work in a blacking (shoe polish) factory. The loneliness and distress

*Charles was born in a terraced house at Portsmouth (below). Later, his father was posted to Chatham dockyards near Rochester (left), where Charles spent the happiest years of his childhood.*

one of the greatest and most popular English novelists of all time. It also established him as a leading champion of the poor, who never ceased to campaign on their behalf.

Dickens was only 24 when his talent as a writer was first widely recognized, but the fame and wealth that came with this success were not able to erase his painful memories of childhood.

He was born in Landport, Portsmouth, on February 7, 1812 and during his very early years he was happy enough. His father, John, was a good-hearted, sociable man. He worked as a clerk in the Navy pay office and in 1817 was transferred to Chatham in Kent after short periods in London and Sheerness. Here young Charles spent five contented years. He liked to read books and

*The publication in serial form of The Pickwick Papers (right) brought Charles fame when he was only 24. Its sales established him as one of the most popular writers of the time. Dickens' brother Augustus mispronounced his own nickname "Moses" as "Boses". It was shortened to "Boz" and later Dickens borrowed it as a pen-name.*

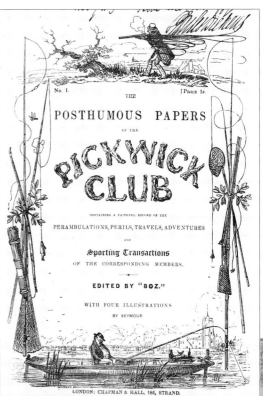

*At 19, Dickens was a shorthand reporter in the House of Commons (above).*

he endured at this time were to haunt his imagination for the rest of his life. Many of his books and his social writings included this boyhood experience, in particular his masterpiece, *David Copperfield*.

After John Dickens was freed from prison, his eldest son's misery at the blacking factory continued. He was to work there for another ten months or so before returning to education. His father made all the arrangements to take Charles out of the blacking factory, but to the boy's utter dismay, his mother was reluctant to let their son leave paid employment. Dickens never forgave his mother for trying to make him stay working in the factory, and later used her as a model for the silly, vain mother in his novel *Nicholas Nickleby*. Charles was then sent to a private school for nearly three years before getting another job, this time as an office boy in a firm of lawyers.

The work was boring, so Dickens, after teaching himself shorthand, set

*Dicken's wife Catherine (left), was the daughter of the music critic on **The Morning Chronicle**. Her sister, Mary, lived with them after their marriage and was the inspiration for the character of Little Nell. Above, the first four of Charles and Catherine's ten children, Charles (center Mary, Kate and Walter (baby). Dickens was probably fondest of Kate.*

*The market at Covent Garden (right) as it would have looked to Dickens on his solitary walks round the poorest parts of London. His books revealed the deplorable side of the city to many of his readers.*

# Dickens in Despair

Two days after his twelfth birthday, Charles reported for work at a boot-blacking factory.

It was a dark, rat-infested building by the River Thames, and his heart sank as he stepped over the threshold.

For six shillings a week he was to paper and label pots of blacking from eight o'clock in the morning until eight at night.

He had been working in the factory for less than two weeks when his father, John, was sent to the Marshalsea debtors' prison.

Charles was desperately lonely. He stayed in lodgings, with barely enough money to buy food.

As an adult he would never forget this time of utter despair and hopelessness.

1824.

**Dickens always kept a china monkey mascot on his desk (above). His public readings of his books (right) were popular wherever he went.**

himself to recording the business of the law courts, and later of the House of Commons. By the age of 23, he was a successful journalist, and moved to a daily newspaper, the *Morning Chronicle*. Shortly before this, he started to write fiction.

In 1833, he sent a semi-fictional account of London life to the *Monthly Magazine*, which ran the story and asked for more. Dickens eagerly supplied these and they were published, along with stories in two daily newspapers, under the pen-name "Boz".

On the day after his 24th birthday, all these writings were published together in a book entitled *Sketches by Boz*. The book was an immediate success and led to a publisher's contract to write a comical story, *The Pickwick Papers*, in 20 monthly instalments of 12,000 words.

Dickens now felt he had enough money to get married, and in 1836 he made Catherine Hogarth his wife. She was a placid, amiable woman who was to have ten children, and be Charles's companion for 22 years. He sometimes complained about her lack of

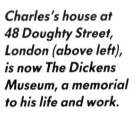

**Charles's house at 48 Doughty Street, London (above left), is now The Dickens Museum, a memorial to his life and work.**

**A prosperous Dickens with his daughters Mary and Kate (standing, above right) at Gad's Hill Place.**

**Charles's friendship with Ellen Ternan (above) caused a great deal of gossip and led to the break-up of his marriage.**

organization and from time to time was dissatisfied with their relationship.

By 1837, Dickens had a good income, for *The Pickwick Papers* sold 40,000 copies a month. He was accepted by London's highest society and regularly visited the mansions of the rich. At the same time, he set to work writing *Oliver Twist*.

In addition to journalistic articles and travel books, Dickens went on to write another 12 major novels and numerous short stories. These contained a vast range of colorful characters who immediately seized the reader's imagination and made Dickens popular in a way no English novelist had been before. *The Old Curiosity Shop*, for example, sold in weekly instalments to over 100,000 people in Britain. In America, its audience was even larger and crowds would wait for the boat to arrive with copies of the latest instalment.

No matter how rich he became, Dickens

**Mourners at Dickens' final resting place (right): Poet's Corner, Westminster Abbey.**

always looked for new projects to work on. In between writing his novels and short stories, he set up and ran two magazines and a national daily newspaper, went on trips to America and Europe, and directed and acted in amateur theatricals. It seems he had so much creative energy, he was never content to stay at home. In 1858, for instance, despite low spirits, he eagerly embarked on a country-wide reading tour.

It was around this time that the unhappiness of his marriage to Catherine finally came out into the open. Dickens had fallen in love with a young actress called Ellen Ternan, and Catherine had expressed her jealousy. This turned Dickens against his wife and they separated in 1858, she to live in London, he to make his chief address Gad's Hill Place, the house in the heart of the Kent countryside that he had wanted for years, and finally bought in 1856.

He returned to this house after his last public reading in 1870, and died there on June 9, while still at work on his last novel, *The Mystery of Edwin Drood*. The mystery was destined to remain unsolved. Dickens' death saddened a world that loved and admired his genius as a storyteller. The American poet Henry Longfellow wrote: "I never knew an author's death to cause such general mourning . . . this whole country is stricken with grief."

# HARD TIMES

*Thomas Barnardo*

**In the mean streets of urban England, life was wretched. Who was there to help?**

*Elizabeth Fry*

*Baroness Burdett-Coutts*

Hulton Picture Company

andering through the streets of London, 12-year-old Charles Dickens saw sights that would haunt him for the rest of his life. He saw people with pale, pinched faces and hungry eyes looking into the shops of the rich. He saw them go home with empty stomachs, to squalid houses. As an adult, he was to campaign tirelessly on their behalf, demanding that the government help the millions who could not help themselves, and improve conditions for the poor.

There were many others who made similar demands. Among them was Elizabeth Fry, the Quaker daughter of a wealthy banker. In 1813, she heard about the appalling conditions in Newgate Prison. Young women and

girls, not yet found guilty of any crime, mixed with criminals so violent that the prison governor himself was afraid to walk among them. Worse still, their children were herded together with them in unhygienic, unhealthy living quarters.

Elizabeth visited the jail to provide practical help. She gave the women clothes, found useful things for them to do, and set up a school for the children. She also campaigned for prison reform generally, so that eventually an inquiry was set up and matters at last began to improve.

It was not only in the prisons that people lived in unhealthy conditions, as was vividly shown in Dickens'

*Unemployment brought starvation to the poor in London. The newly formed Salvation Army launched a social campaign (far right) in an effort to improve conditions. For some of the hungry, relief came from food left over from the annual Lord Mayor's Banquet (right).*

Fine Art Photographic Library

Mary Evans

33

novels. This view was backed up in 1842 by Edwin Chadwick, a civil servant and associate and correspondent of Charles Dickens, who discovered that cholera, a deadly disease, was most likely to strike wherever people lived in filthy surroundings.

In the big towns, the back streets were often piled high with rubbish, including human excrement. On either side were dark, dank buildings, each room housing one or two families. These families rarely breathed fresh air or drank clean water, and one of their number was likely to die almost every year.

Chadwick argued that the government should act to improve the health of such families. At the very least, he insisted, a committee responsible for sanitary matters such as sewerage, drainage, cleaning and paving should be set up in every town. The government eventually took up some of his ideas and set up a National Board of Health for England and Wales.

With Chadwick on this new board was Lord Shaftesbury, a rich aristocrat who devoted his whole life to fighting for the poor, particularly for children. He had had an unhappy childhood himself, neglected by his parents and bullied at school, which might explain his interest in disadvantaged children. Whatever the reason, he was responsible for getting the first Factory

Graham Humphries

*A CHIMNEY SWEEP (above right), A DEBTOR'S PRISON (below)*

Act through Parliament in 1833. After that he became involved with every measure concerned with the welfare of children.

The first Factory Act made it illegal for children under the age of nine to be employed in a cotton, woolen or flax mill. Children under 13 were not to be employed for more than 48 hours a week, and children from 13 to 18 for no more than 69 hours a week. At a time when young children were often forced to work 16 hours a day in appalling conditions, this Act was very important. It showed that the government accepted some responsibility for the way factories were run, and realized that it must help the weak and defenceless.

Among those who desperately needed the government's help were the women and children who worked in the coal mines. Here they pushed, dragged and carried the coal, being forced to stay below ground, in almost total darkness, for 14 hours a day or sometimes longer. Lord Shaftesbury ensured that

from 1842 an Act of Parliament forbad their employment in the mines.

Another group who were put to work in darkness were the chimney sweeps, young boys who were beaten and made to climb up long, soot-choked flues. Many lost limbs,

# THE VICTORIAN WATER

*Waterborne diseases were widespread in London before it became law for each house to have a fixed sanitary arrangement. The death of Prince Albert from typhoid gave the biggest impetus to sanitary development; a design was produced which is still the basis for modern flush toilets.*

**The washdown bowl (left) rinses with every flush, while the U-bend prevents smells drifting back. The washout closet (right) lost popularity in England but is still widely used on the Continent.**

**During the 1850s, houses up-river were desirable, as the Thames was both London's water source and its sewer. This made the river a carrier of death and disease, as seen in this cartoon (left).**

**Terracotta pipes (below) connected the flush toilets to the sewer systems, completed in London in 1865 and originally draining into the Thames.**

JENNINGS' IMPROVED

were badly burned or even died. Charles Kingsley, a Church of England clergyman, took up the chimney sweeps' cause and wrote about them in a novel, *The Water Babies,* published in 1863. Lord Shaftesbury used the publicity from this book to persuade the government to pass an Act which stopped boys being forced to climb chimneys.

One of Lord Shaftesbury's friends was an

*For the poor, alcohol was often the only way to escape from their misery. Gin palaces (above) were cheap and begging (left) could provide the necessary money. Diseases were still little understood and children were likely victims. Even those whose parents could afford a doctor (below) were far from certain to survive – treatment was often simply not available.*

Irish medical student, Thomas Barnardo, who wanted to be a medical missionary in China. On coming to London, he found the streets swarming with dirty, hungry and neglected children and decided to open a "ragged school". This type of school had first been set up in the 1830s by a group of religious people who wanted to offer a little education to some of the poorest children. Barnardo soon discovered that many of these children were homeless, so he set up a mission in London where they could sleep. He decided to stay in England, rather than go to China, when he was promised £1000 to open a home for destitute boys. This was started in 1870, and was to be the first of many, for both boys and girls.

Another person involved in setting up ragged schools was Angela Burdett-Coutts. The granddaughter of a wealthy banker, she came into a vast inheritance when she was 23 and used the money to support good causes. She became a friend of Charles Dickens, and together they set up a refuge for women who wished to escape from prostitution.

For Dickens, such a venture was just one very small part of a life-long campaign on behalf of the poor. Their misery and appalling living conditions were made known to a wide public through his books, described in heart-breaking detail. But he was not satisfied just with putting pen to paper, and backed up his words with actions.

Colin Salmon

Fotomas

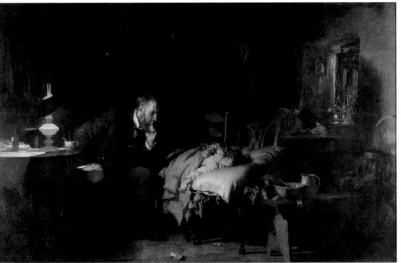

E T Archivo/Tate Gallery

# JOLLY FINE BOATING WEATHER

**On the playing fields of Eton, a young schoolboy learns how to become a fine Victorian gentleman.**

have been looking forward to this day for weeks! It's the Fourth of June, the anniversary of the birth of George III and the day when, every year, there is a procession of boats rowed down the Thames by Eton boys. Traditionally the crews dress up as sailors, with the coxes in the uniforms of midshipmen or admirals. It is meant to be formal and proper, but usually the down-river procession turns into a bumping race. It's all great fun!

My family are watching in the crowd. My mother and sisters have had new dresses and bonnets made specially for the occasion. My younger brother can hardly contain his excitement – he keeps asking about the band and the cricket and the fireworks, and wants to know

David Cuzik

why I'm not rowing in one of the boats.

Personally, I'm not too keen on rowing, although many of the boys practice hard to get into the school's rowing eight. I would much rather play a good game of cricket or, in winter, football. They're both games to which we devote a lot of time at Eton. The masters know how important it is for all young gentlemen to acquire team spirit; they realize this will have an important effect on the way we behave later in life, when we will be responsible for governing and leading the nation.

Actually, I think it very unlikely that I shall go into government. My father is the owner of a textile factory and I shall join him in the business when I've finished my education, and eventually inherit it.

Some people might say that Eton is an odd choice of school to send me to. After all, when we're not playing sport, we're studying works written in Latin and Greek, and these aren't going to be much use in a factory. The only way I can learn about science or mathematics is for my father to make special arrangements and pay extra fees for me to do so. My father is a self-made man who became successful through sheer hard work, and he is very proud that his son now mixes with aristocrats.

I lodge in one of the boarding houses for Eton College boys which are dotted around the area. They are run either by masters at the school or by women known as "dames". (Apparently Charles Dickens Junior, son of the famous novelist, lodged in the same boarding house when he was a pupil at the school some years ago.)

As a junior, I'm often bullied by the senior boys. They are responsible for discipline in the school and they frequently punish us younger ones by beating us with a cane. I now have to "fag" for one of the seniors, which means I do all his chores, such as making

# NEW POLICE

**With the increase in crime, new measures were needed to combat it.**

Mary Evans Picture Library

**Forerunners of the Metropolitan Police: a watchman (above) and a Bow Street Runner (right).**

Mary Evans Picture Library

Mansell Collection

**Sir Robert Peel (above) founded the Metropolitan Police in 1829, when he was Home Secretary.**

**The Black Maria (right) may have derived its name from Maria Lee, a large black woman who lived in Boston, Mass. The police sent for "Black Maria" when they needed help.**

**One of Sir Robert's "Peelers" (below right) goes about his duty. There was much fierce opposition to the setting up of a police force and when the constables appeared on the streets, they were insulted and even openly jeered at.**

Illustrated London News

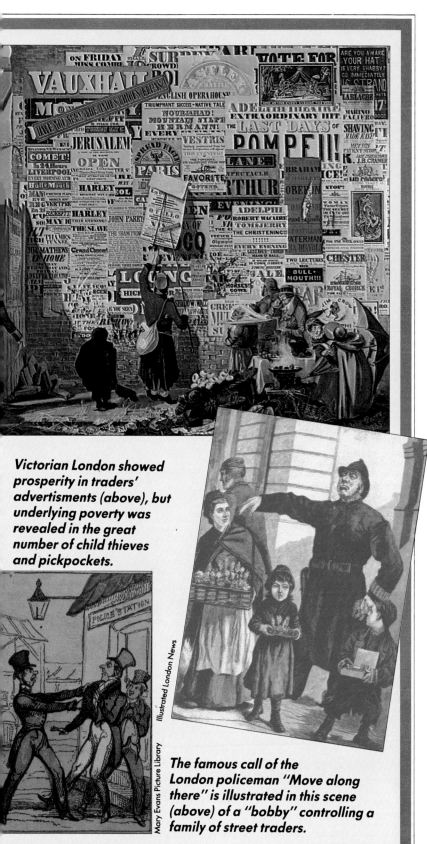

Victorian London showed prosperity in traders' advertisments (above), but underlying poverty was revealed in the great number of child thieves and pickpockets.

*Illustrated London News*

*Mary Evans Picture Library*

The famous call of the London policeman "Move along there" is illustrated in this scene (above) of a "bobby" controlling a family of street traders.

tea and lighting the fire. Also, I have constantly to run errands for him. I hate it, but in a few years' time I'll be a senior with a junior fagging for me. I must say, however, that I am lucky as my fagmaster is not a bad chap and, on the whole, is rather decent to me. Things could be a lot worse.

I know that life is much the same in the other top public schools. I've often heard my father discussing them with his friends, and it seems that all the schools teach little besides Latin and Greek. Science, history, mathematics and foreign languages are all regarded as inferior subjects. One of my father's friends says this is disgraceful because these are exactly the subjects which boys in this day and age should be studying. He says the grammar schools aren't much better and it's time some new schools were established. Perhaps, when I grow up, I'll send my sons to one of these new schools.

Educating one's daughters is another matter entirely. Girls in wealthy families are usually taught at home by governesses and, in any case, they are not expected to study serious subjects. My sisters, however, do a little reading and writing between sessions of drawing, sewing and playing the piano.

One of their friends attends the recently founded Cheltenham Ladies' College, where education is taken a lot more seriously. My father is quite horrified by this and says his daughters need know nothing more than how to provide pleasant company and run a household properly.

My sisters are, nevertheless, a lot better educated than the children who work in my father's factory. Many of them have never been to school at all and do not know how to read or write. It seems their parents cannot afford even the few pennies needed to send them to one of the schools for the poor.

Apparently, in these places as many as 500 boys and girls are taught together in one large room and the noise can be deafening. The teacher appoints some of the older children as "monitors" and uses them to help teach the younger ones. The monitors go up to the platform where the teacher sits, are taught a skill such as how to spell a

# COUNTRY CONTRASTS

As farming became mechanized, horses and men (above) were replaced by steam engines (below).

Despite romantic ideas of rural life (left), the reality was different. The agricultural worker and his family (above), often lived in abject poverty and deprivation.

Community activities, such as dancing on the village green (right), were gradually lost as rural workers left the land for the mines and factories.

particular word, then each goes back to a group of ten children and passes on that skill. It sounds even more tedious than translating big chunks of Latin and Greek, but it's really the best these children can hope for.

The government gives some money to these schools every year, but I've heard my father's friend say that it's nowhere near enough. He says the government should pay for all children to go to school, at least until they are 11 years old, so that everyone will be able to read and write. My father argues with him and says that people should look after themselves rather than relying on the government to improve their lives. He frequently quotes the words of Samuel Smiles, who wrote, "Heaven helps those who help themselves." His book is very popular, so I think a lot of people must agree with him. Actually, I rather agree with my father's friend.

I don't know who is right, but I'm sure about one thing – a lot of people are talking about education and changes will be made by the time I've grown up. Oh yes, and there's another thing I'm sure about: the boys of Eton College will continue to celebrate the Fourth of June for many years to come!

# Vincent

# van Gogh

**B**eing an artist was not van Gogh's first choice. He began his working life as an art dealer and then a teacher in London. His father, a pastor, had taught his children the ideals of service and personal sacrifice. It was witnessing the appalling lives of London's poor that reminded Vincent of these ideals. He became a pastor too, dedicated to helping others. However, his lifelong emotional instability led to his contract not being renewed. One of the world's greatest artists turned to painting as a last, desperate resort when his church rejected him.

# Vincent

## Rejected by society and his church, Vincent van Gogh expressed his lonely, passionate nature in paint.

Bridgeman/Rijksmuseum Kröller-Müller, Otterlo

incent van Gogh was born on March 30 1853, in Groot Zundert, a small Dutch village near the Belgian border. He was one of six children and his birth came one year to the day after his mother had given birth to a stillborn son. This boy had also been called Vincent, which meant that, every time van Gogh passed through the local churchyard, he could see a gravestone with his name and birthday inscribed on it.

Van Gogh's father was a pastor in the Dutch Reformed Church and Vincent's character was shaped by religious ideals of service and sincerity, combined with the austere discipline of a Protestant upbringing. As a child, he was sullen and withdrawn, never happier than when he was gathering plants and birds' nests by himself in the countryside. From an early age, however, van Gogh was also fond of sketching and his father used to give away his son's drawings as prizes to his best Sunday school pupils.

One of the boy's uncles – yet another Vincent! – was a successful art dealer and, through him, van Gogh gained his first job at The Hague branch of Goupil & Co, selling drawings and paintings. He remained with the firm for

*In the little Dutch village of Zundert, Vincent's father was the preacher at this church (below) and Vincent's eldest brother was buried there.*

Vincent van Gogh Foundation, Van Gogh Museum Amsterdam

## Personal Profile

**VINCENT VAN GOGH**
**Born** *March 30, 1853*
**Died** *July 29, 1890*
**Parents** *Reverend Theodorus van Gogh and Anna Carbentus*
**Personal appearance** *He had red hair and usually wore a beard. He was broadly built, with a slight stoop and had a ruddy complexion and deep-set, piercing blue eyes.*
**General** *He had very high ideals and was deeply moved by other people's suffering, but was intense, uncompromising and had a fiery temper. Had difficulty in keeping close friends due to his moodiness and instability, but longed for love and recognition.*

Vincent's grandfather and his father (right) were parsons in the Dutch Reformed Church. Vincent absorbed a sense of service from his family and was affected by the hardships and suffering of others.

Anna van Gogh (left) wrote and painted and Vincent inherited his artistic abilities from her. But, though as a small boy he was fond of drawing, his mother did not give him special encouragement.

seven years, working in Brussels, London and Paris. Vincent's work gave him a good background knowledge of art, but he was essentially ill-suited to the regularity and controlled manners of business life, and abandoned his career with Goupil's in 1876.

When he stopped working as an art dealer, he determined to follow a quite different course in life – one that would fulfil early ideals of service and sacrifice. He had worked for a short period as a teacher on the outskirts of London, where he witnessed the squalor of living in the poorer parts of the city, and this filled him with a sense of mission. Thus inspired, he decided to follow his father's example and study for the priest-

*Theo van Gogh (above) was a devoted brother. He helped Vincent with money and gave the artist every support in his work. Vincent was able to rent this little room in Arles (below) with Theo's financial help and the warm glow of the painting reveals Vincent's happy mood in this period of his life.*

flock, if his ministry was to be successful. He lived in a primitive hut, where he slept on straw and ate very little. He gave away his warm clothing and sided with the miners in a strike. Not surprisingly, the inspectors of the mission felt that this was taking the message of the Bible too literally and, after six months, they refused to renew his contract.

Vincent was distraught at the Church's rejection of his work, but he remained in the area until 1880, working without payment. During this time, he began to make sketches of the local miners, weavers and peasants and it gradually occurred to him that he should make art his career. The zeal and

| 1750 | 1800 | 1850 | 1900 | 1950 | 2000 |
|------|------|------|------|------|------|

Napoleon
Beethoven
Abraham Lincoln
Charles Darwin
Charles Dickens
David Livingstone
Karl Marx
Queen Victoria
Florence Nightingale
Louis Pasteur
William Cody
Vincent van Gogh

## THEIR PLACE IN HISTORY

hood, and in 1877 became a student at an evangelical school for preachers.

The academic discipline of the course frustrated Vincent and, with his father's help, he moved to the Borinage, a bleak coal-mining area in southern Belgium, where he took up lay preaching.

Here, again, his intensity gave his colleagues cause for concern. Van Gogh believed that he had to share the sufferings of his

*Vincent fell madly in love with Kee Vos-Stricker (left), a widow with a son. To try to force her to see him, Vincent put his hand in the flame of a lamp, but she would not relent and he had to be saved from burning himself. His fierce emotions scared most women.*

intensity that van Gogh had poured into religious service was now transferred to his new passion—to be an artist.

His parents allowed him to use a building adjoining the vicarage as a studio, but Vincent's chief support came from his younger brother, Theo. For years, this beloved brother paid for his upkeep and sent him money for painting materials. He was also an unfailing source of encouragement during the many periods when Vincent's lack of recognition left him prey to self-doubt and uncertainty. The two brothers corresponded regularly from 1872 until Vincent's death. This powerful

**The hardships of the coalminers in the Borinage (above) were captured in Vincent's earlier works.**

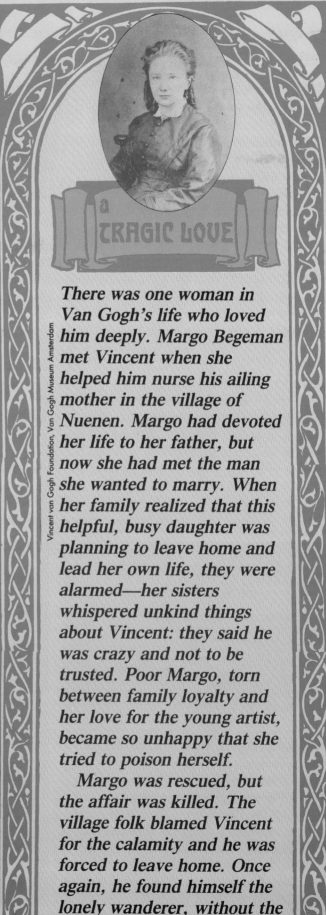

## a TRAGIC LOVE

There was one woman in Van Gogh's life who loved him deeply. Margo Begeman met Vincent when she helped him nurse his ailing mother in the village of Nuenen. Margo had devoted her life to her father, but now she had met the man she wanted to marry. When her family realized that this helpful, busy daughter was planning to leave home and lead her own life, they were alarmed—her sisters whispered unkind things about Vincent: they said he was crazy and not to be trusted. Poor Margo, torn between family loyalty and her love for the young artist, became so unhappy that she tried to poison herself.

Margo was rescued, but the affair was killed. The village folk blamed Vincent for the calamity and he was forced to leave home. Once again, he found himself the lonely wanderer, without the comfort of love.

1884

*Van Gogh returned to his parents in 1883, after a miserable time in The Hague. He began to paint local scenes using dark colors, symbolic of the earth. From this period came* **The Potato Eaters** *(right), an emotional painting which shows his pity for the hard lives of rural people. But in Paris, in 1886, he learnt to use lighter colors as in* **The Sunflowers** *(below).*

Vincent van Gogh Foundation, Van Gogh Museum Amsterdam

Vincent van Gogh Foundation, Van Gogh Museum Amsterdam

bond with Theo was vital to van Gogh, the painter.

Vincent's artistic training was haphazard. Initially, he was self-taught, working from copy-book examples of Holbein drawings and the woodcuts of Millet. He received some tuition from his cousin's husband, Anton Mauve, and studied briefly at the art academy in Antwerp. It was only after he moved to Paris in 1886, however, that he began to develop the technique and ideas that were to reach such brilliant expression in the last five years of his life. Here, in the artistic capital of Europe, van Gogh was able to mix with the leading painters of the day, learning from their example. He found that the artists of Paris were in a state of liberation, having been freed from the constraints of the Academy of Fine Arts in France by the work of the Impressionists. These painters had created a new awareness of color and had developed a thick, graphic brush style in their painting technique. Vincent also learnt to paint out of doors, straight from nature, and not to perfect his canvasses in the studio.

Paris offered van Gogh a rare interlude of companionship in a life that otherwise tended to be full of loneliness and isolation. Even here, however, his bursts of temper and his tactless behavior made him into an outsider and, in February 1888, he moved to Arles, in the south of France.

Vincent's early months in his new home were very happy. He worked extremely hard and managed to make friends with some of the locals, such as Roulin the

postmaster and a soldier called Milliet. His greatest wish however was to set up an artistic colony and, to this end, he persuaded a friend from Paris, the painter Paul Gauguin, to leave the capital, and come to live with him in his yellow house in Arles.

It was a disastrous move. Within two months, they had quarreled violently and, in December 1888, during a bitter and drunken exchange between the two artists, van Gogh cut off a corner of his own ear lobe. Gauguin fled back to Paris and Vincent was confined briefly to a cell in Arles Hospital. Van Gogh was to spend the remainder of his life under the oppressive shadow of mental instability and illness.

*The Yellow House in Arles (above) to which Vincent invited Gauguin. Yellow is symbolic of friendship and van Gogh delighted in using this color for his home.*

*In 1889, Vincent went into a mental hospital (left) in Saint-Remy-de-Provence. The place was partly a refuge for this sad artist. He stayed here for about one year. Theo then put him in the care of Dr Gachet (inset) who was also an artist. Van Gogh's last portrait was of this doctor.*

*After Vincent had shot himself, Theo rushed to his brother and nursed him through the last hours. Six months later Theo, too, was dead. The brothers are buried side by side in the graveyard at Auvers-sur-Oise (right)—a gentle testimony to their affection.*

This illness was at the time diagnosed as a form of epilepsy, and later as schizophrenia. In 1889, he voluntarily entered the asylum at nearby Saint-Remy. There he worked frantically between his attacks of insanity. These paintings from Arles developed beyond the ideas of Impressionism. The Impressionists' use of clear color was transformed by van Gogh into color as an expression of emotion, and his brush work was used not to enhance complementary colors, as the Impressionists intended, but to indicate shape, form and outline.

In 1890, Vincent moved to Auvers, but was unable to shake off his loneliness and depression. He shot himself on July 27 and died two days later. Theo also died prematurely, in 1891, and the two brothers were eventually buried side by side.

# The Impressionists

**When they fused art with a scientific view of color, Impressionists created a revolution in painting and changed the vision of Europe.**

*As an Impressionist, Cézanne (above) took to painting nature. But he slowly developed his own technique using bold, square brushstrokes, which earned him the grand title of "father of modern art".*

*Manet's Déjeuner sur l'herbe (right) was exhibited in 1863 and caused an uproar. Its subject matter of a naked woman sitting with two fully clothed modern men shocked the public. Almost as offensive was the free painting style, and bright colors, instead of the dark, gloomy ones approved by the Academy.*

During the nineteenth century, a small group of painters living in Paris found a new way of looking at the world and new ways of painting it. Without the work of this group, called the Impressionists, the direction and development of painting in our own times would have been quite different.

It was their revolutionary understanding of color, expressed through thick, broken brushstrokes, that allowed van Gogh to emerge as a great, unique talent. Their principle of painting direct from nature allowed van Gogh his eccentric habit of painting outside at night. With candles stuck to his hat, this artist made his own intense exploration of light and nature.

For centuries, artists and their methods of work, or technique, had been controlled in France by the Academy of Fine Arts. Even the social upheaval of the French Revolution in 1789 had hardly altered the rigid "rules of art" devised by the men who ran the Academy. Indeed, Jacques Louis David, who in 1799 was given control of the Academy, insisted on a Neo-Classical approach to painting and this was continued by his successor, Jean Ingres. This meant that artists were expected to include classical themes from Greek and Roman art in their work and were encouraged to paint heroic or religious subjects. Even landscapes had to contain mythological elements.

The Academy regulated painting techniques as well as the subject matter. Paint was applied in smooth, even brushstrokes in what was called a "licked" surface, and light and shade were not expected to be realistic,

*Renoir (above) expressed his love of life in his paintings filled with warm colors. By 40, he had gained recognition through his society portraits.*

49

but were "arranged" for dramatic effect. All painting
was contrived and completed in the studio.

A few painters rebelled against the Academy. Jean
Millet (1814-75) and Gustave Courbet (1819-77) in
France painted pictures of peasants and working people
in everyday contemporary life, and William Turner
(1775-1851) and John Constable (1776-1837) in
England, painted landscapes without contriving artifi-
cial drama. But even they used traditional techniques
in their brushwork, and their use of color
generally followed orthodox rules.

Malcolm Chandler

50

Mary Evans

**A horse in motion (above), and an 1870's photographer (below).**

Hulton Picture Library

The Academy took no interest in the extraordinary technical and scientific advances of contemporary society, but the artists who were to become the leaders of Impressionism were excited by all the new knowledge. In 1839, Eugene Chevreul had written a book about the principles of harmony and contrast in colors. For the first time, a methodical analysis of color had been attempted, and this work was extended by other scientists, who found a way of working on color broken through a prism, in a device called the spectrograph.

The Impressionists subscribed to scientific magazines and many of their discussions in the cafés were about light and color. They determined to capture the shifting moods of color in light and shadow, and to do this they moved their easels outside and painted from nature. The Academy was shocked by such "undisciplined" painting!

Technology had invented the camera and the new photographers cried, "Now painting is dead!" Photographic images, however, actually inspired the Impressionists. Focus was altered in photographs, and movement was accurately recorded. For instance, until the camera showed otherwise, everyone thought that a galloping horse lifted all four feet off the ground, with the front legs forwards and the back legs flung behind.

Foreign travel and exploration also brought artistic revelations. Japanese prints had come into Europe after the Americans entered Japan in 1853. Before this date, the warrior society of Japan had been closed to

# The Japanese Influence

Giraudon/Galerie J. Ostier, Paris

**Cheap Japanese woodblock prints (above) arrived in Europe on ships from the Orient, used as packing material.**

Vincent van Gogh Foundation, Van Gogh Museum Amsterdam

*The composition and perspective in Japanese prints were quite different from those used by European artists. Japanese artists chose everyday subjects and scenes which were portrayed with childlike simplicity and charm. Generally available in France from the mid-1850s, they must have seemed exciting to van Gogh and Gauguin.*

Giraudon/Galerie J. Ostier, Paris

**Van Gogh, like other artists, studied Japanese prints (left) . In a frank imitation of this Oriental style he so admired, van Gogh painted this scene (center) complete with decorative border.**

outsiders for centuries, and very little of its art had reached the West. European artists were startled by the flat colors and geometric compositions of these prints.

The Impressionists—Manet, Monet, Renoir, Pissarro, Degas, Cézanne and Sisley—developed as young students their technical and scientific knowledge, but their work was broken by the Franco-Prussian War in 1870-71. When the war ended, the group rejoined, but Paris was no longer their center. Monet continued working and living in the country, trying to capture the natural light in the landscape. Degas preferred Paris life and the effects of gas and electric light. All, however, were agreed on their revolutionary understanding of color. The Impressionists understood the visual effects of complementary colors, such as "Red, the complementary of green, being placed next to green, increases the intensity of green." So they painted pure color in thick brushstrokes, one against the other, and relied on the scientifically analyzed effect of this on the eye; in doing this they totally disregarded the old mixed tones and "licked" surface of the Academy. They disregarded, too,

*Lauros-Giraudon/Musée d'Orsay, Paris*

*In **Le Moulin de la Galette**, (above) Renoir captures moments of fun at a café. The people are dappled with light filtering through trees.*

the academic subject matter and love of classical references. Their preferred subjects were the natural landscape and ordinary people.

The Impressionists were reviled, abused and laughed at in their first exhibitions, but their concept of color and composition created a revolution in Western painting.

*Edimage*

*Monet was the first to use the word "impression" as a title to his work,* Impression: Sunrise, *a view of Le Havre harbor (above).*

*Dance Class by Degas (right) has the freshness of a photograph. It was shown at the first Impressionist exhibition in 1874.*

*Lauros-Giraudon/Musée d'Orsay, Paris*

53

# BOHEMIAN PARIS

## The most glamorous and exciting city in 19th century Europe, Paris was a magnet for artists, entertainers and the wealthy.

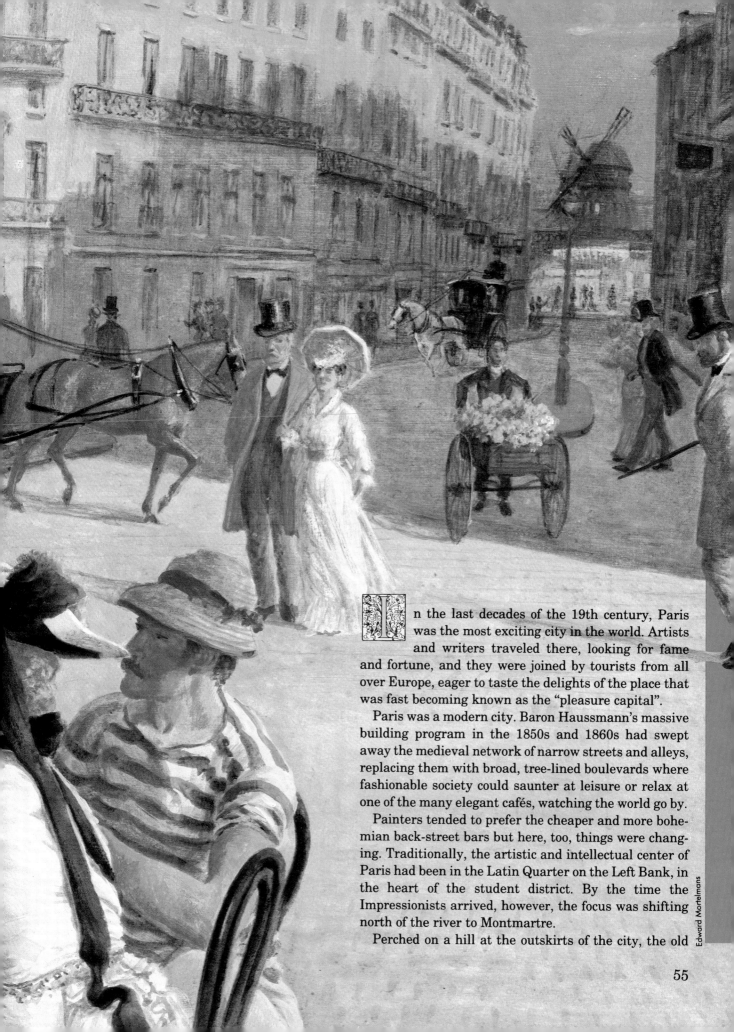

In the last decades of the 19th century, Paris was the most exciting city in the world. Artists and writers traveled there, looking for fame and fortune, and they were joined by tourists from all over Europe, eager to taste the delights of the place that was fast becoming known as the "pleasure capital".

Paris was a modern city. Baron Haussmann's massive building program in the 1850s and 1860s had swept away the medieval network of narrow streets and alleys, replacing them with broad, tree-lined boulevards where fashionable society could saunter at leisure or relax at one of the many elegant cafés, watching the world go by.

Painters tended to prefer the cheaper and more bohemian back-street bars but here, too, things were changing. Traditionally, the artistic and intellectual center of Paris had been in the Latin Quarter on the Left Bank, in the heart of the student district. By the time the Impressionists arrived, however, the focus was shifting north of the river to Montmartre.

Perched on a hill at the outskirts of the city, the old

Edward Mortelmans

55

windmills of Montmartre gave the suburb a semi-rural character. For artists, though, the main attractions were the very low cost of renting studios and the presence of numerous minor art dealers, who could be persuaded to sell the work of unknown or new artists.

Another advantage of the area was that the seedy but animated district of Pigalle lay nearby, at the foot of the hill. There, poor artists could exchange their paintings for lodgings or food, while the local theaters, bars and brothels provided an unsurpassed night-life which drew visitors from all parts of the city.

The artistic life of Paris revolved round the cafés. Here, painters and writers could meet to discuss their work in pleasant and informal surroundings. This gave an important sense of community to artists who were unable to sell their pictures and who might otherwise have felt very isolated. The Impressionists, for example, used to meet regularly at the Café Guerbois or the Café Nouvelle-Athènes.

Sometimes, the café owners allowed their customers to hold small shows on the premises. In 1887, van Gogh, Toulouse-Lautrec and Bernard staged joint exhibitions, and the best known of these was held in Le Tambourin café in the Boulevard de Clichy.

The café meetings were not confined to painters. Poets, journalists and critics were also frequently present and these contacts did much to enrich Parisian culture. For example, the novelist Zola was a childhood friend of Paul Cézanne and wrote many articles in defence of the Impressionists. The poet Baudelaire was equally supportive of Manet and his fellow painters, urging them to use their talents to show modern life.

The Impressionists have left us with a very vivid record of the various entertainments that were on offer in Paris. The most colorful of these were the cabarets and the nightclubs; places like Le Chat Noir (the Black Cat), which was opened by a failed artist and which, as Le Mirliton, became the regular venue for Aristide Bruant, the singer immortalized in Lautrec's posters. Even more famous was the Moulin Rouge (the Red Windmill), a notorious dance-hall which combined both the sleazier and the more glamorous aspects of Parisian night-life.

The interior of the Moulin Rouge was very plush, and boisterous entertainment included cancan dancers, singers and acrobats. Outside, in the garden, there was a huge wooden elephant, housing an orchestra, and guests could sit and listen to the music.

The Moulin Rouge was patronized by the rich and famous. The colorful, lively atmosphere also appealed to

## FLASH BACK

# THE CHANGING FACE OF FRANCE

*France became an industrialized nation in the 19th century, celebrated by the World Fairs in Paris and a monument to engineering, the Eiffel Tower.*

*Night-time Montmartre became a popular place for artists and rich pleasure-seekers alike. The Moulin Rouge dance-hall (above) was famous for its cancan dancers. The first bicycle show was held in Paris and the first cycle race (Paris to Rouen) took place in 1869. Cycling became a popular pastime for women in the 1890s (right).*

France declared war on Prussia in 1870 (right). The dispute was over the German candidate for the Spanish throne. The French were afraid of an increase in Prussian power, but the French army was defeated and Paris besieged. The Treaty of Frankfurt, 1871, was harsh on France who had to pay a large indemnity to the Germans.

Alexandre Gustave Eiffel (below) was France's best-known engineer. Apart from his tower, he designed the structure of the Statue of Liberty and the Panama Canal locks.

When the poverty-stricken people of Paris were cold and hungry in the winter of 1871, they defied the government, started an uprising, (above) and decided to govern themselves by proclaiming a Commune.

The Paris skyline is dominated by the Eiffel Tower (right), constructed for the Exhibitions of 1889. Built of steel girders it is 1,056 feet (322 meters) high.

A series of Paris Exhibitions, starting in 1855, were held to demonstrate the rapid progress of French industry. The 1878 Exhibition (above) was, until then, the largest world fair ever held, with 52,000 exhibits attracting 16 million visitors.

artists such as Henri Toulouse-Lautrec, who was the eccentric son of a French nobleman. In 1890, Henri, who was a cripple, was so enraged by another artist who dared to criticize van Gogh, that he challenged the man to a duel!

But the colorful and picturesque could be found all over Paris. Seurat favored Fernando's circus in Montmartre, with its bareback riders and its trapeze artists, while Degas' paintings revealed his fascination with ballet performances and classes. Also, ballet dancers were not considered entirely respectable, and Degas, as an Impressionist, wished to study and record all aspects of contemporary life. He also adored the horse-races for similar reasons.

Electric lighting first appeared in Paris in 1889. This was just one of the many signs of the technical achievements of the 19th century. The invention of the pneumatic tyre in 1888 helped to make cycling a popular pastime, while the working model of Panhard and Levassor's motor car, which was completed five years later, pointed the way to future developments. The métro did not appear until the last years of the century, but by the 1860s and 1870s the expansion of the railways brought the surrounding countryside within easy reach. Artists flocked to riverside beauty spots like Argenteuil and La Grenouillère which were painted by Monet and Renoir. There, they could watch regattas, try their hand at boating or simply pass the time in one of the open-air cafés.

However, the most enduring symbol of this magical period in Paris's history was the Eiffel Tower. Built as the showpiece of the city's fourth Universal Exhibition, the Tower met with some disapproval at first. A professor of mathematics predicted that it would collapse if it rose above 700 feet (212 meters) and a petition was drawn up by its critics, comparing it to a "gigantic, black factory chimney". Happily their objections were ignored and Paris's most famous landmark was completed in 1889.

# Van Gogh's Holland

*Holland, during van Gogh's life, was a prosperous, conservative country which tolerated the growth of radical ideas in art and design.*

*In the 19th century, country folk often wore traditional clothes. Even now, in parts of Holland, these clothes (right) are worn by some people for religious reasons.*

Mary Evans

Tony Craddock/Tony Stone Worldwide

*For centuries the marshy land was drained with the help of windmills (left) and they are a familiar aspect of the Dutch scene.*

*The pottery works at Delft are famous for their ceramic ware (left), a skill particularly associated with Dutch craftsmen.*

Bridgeman/Victoria & Albert Museum

David Hanson/Tony Stone Worldwide

*The tall, narrow houses so typical of Amsterdam (right) have a simple classical severity, well suited to Dutch taste, and to this city, tightly fitted round canal waterways.*

# GLOSSARY

**abdicate** To formally give up a throne.

**academic** Someone who teaches at a college or university.

**aristocracy** The most privileged class. Those people possessing land and titles as a result of being born into landowning families.

**austere** Basic, with very few comforts.

**bard** A Celtic word for poet, playwright or minstrel.

**Black Maria** A vehicle used by the police to transport prisoners.

**blacking** Boot polish.

**boarding house** A house where a bed and meals are provided in exchange for money.

**bobby** English slang term for a policeman.

**bohemian** A person living in an unconventional way. Usually used to describe the free and easy lifestyle of artists and writers.

**boulevard** A broad avenue which is often lined with trees.

**brothels** Houses in which prostitutes ply their trade.

**cancan** A wild, energetic dance featuring much high kicking.

**Celtic** Originating with the ancient peoples of Scotland, Ireland, Wales or Brittany.

**chamber pot** A pot with a handle used as a portable toilet.

**chimney sweep** Someone whose job is to keep chimneys free of soot.

**cholera** A serious infectious disease, often deadly, which flourishes in insanitary conditions.

**civil servant** An employee of the government who works in administration.

**concerto** A musical composition, usually in three movements, played by a soloist with an orchestra.

**constable** The lowest rank in the English police.

**cox** Someone who steers a small boat.

**cricket** English national game.

**debtor's prison** A prison set aside for people who could not pay money that they owed. The debtor stayed in prison until the debt was paid or the person to whom they owed money died.

**destitute** Without any money or property.

**discreet** Understated, not excessive or showy.

**dynasty** A family line in which power is handed down from generation to generation.

**epilepsy** A nervous disorder which causes the sufferer to have convulsive fits, usually with loss of consciousness.

**excrement** Waste products discharged from the body.

**flax** A plant grown for it seeds and fibers, which are woven into a cloth called linen.

**flues** The smoke ducts of chimneys.

**governess** A private teacher employed to teach children at home.

**grammar school** A school for children over 11 years of age. Most children would have to pass an examination to enter such a school, others would pay to go there. It offered education suitable for professions such as law or medicine.

**grenadiers** Members of the Grenadier Guards, a British infantry regiment.

**guerrilla campaign** A series of surpise raids on an enemy's communication and supply lines by a small group of independent soldiers.

**Home Secretary** British government minister responsible for the law, security and the police force, among other duties. One of the four top political posts in Britain.

**House of Commons** The elected part of the British goverment, roughly the equivalent of the American House of Representatives.

**indemnity** Protection or security against damage or loss.

**librettist** The person who writes the words that go with the music in an opera.

**manuscript** A book, document, letter or musical score written by hand.

**medieval** In the style or fashion of the Middle Ages.

**mentor** A wise and trusted counselor; someone who helps and advises a younger man in his career.

**métro** Subway system in Paris.

**midshipman** The lowest officer rank in the British Navy.

**mythological** Based on traditional stories, particularly of the ancient Romans and Greeks.

**orthodox** Generally accepted as correct; according to the conventions of the day.

**overture** A piece of orchestral music which introduces an opera or ballet.

**prism** A piece of glass, triangular in cross-section, which separates white light into the full spectrum of colors.

**public school** In England, a private, fee-paying school.

**Quaker** A member of a Christian sect properly called the Society of Friends.

**regatta** A series of boat races.

**schizophrenia** A mental disorder. Sufferers can have hallucinations and receive instructions and opinions from imaginary voices.

**sonata** A musical composition for one or two instruments in three or four parts or movements. Each movement has contrasting moods and keys.

**spectrograph** A photograph or drawing of a spectrum.

**superlative** Of the highest order, surpassing all others.

**symphony** An elaborate instrumental composition in three or more movements written for an orchestra.

**terraced house** One of a row of houses built in a rank with no spaces between one house and the next.

**terracotta** Fine quality, unglazed earthenware, reddish brown in color.

**variations** In music, changes or elaborations on a theme or melody.

**venue** The place which is the scene of any action or event.

**viola** A four-stringed instrument belonging to the violin family.

# CHRONOLOGY

## Giants of the Arts 1750 to 1900

|  | POLITICS AND WAR | ART AND PHILOSOPHY |
|---|---|---|
| **1750 to 1780** | **1756-1663** Seven Years' War. England and Prussia fight France and Austria. At Peace of Paris, Prussia gains Silesia and England, Canada.<br>**1762** Catherine the Great becomes Tsarina of Russia.<br>**1765** Josef II becomes Holy Roman Emperor.<br>**1776** American Declaration of Independence. | **1755-72** Publication of French *Encyclopedia*.<br>**1755** Doctor Johnson's *Dictionary of the English Language*.<br>**1759** Death of Handel. Haydn's *First Symphony*.<br>**1771** First edition of the *Encylopedia Britannica*.<br>**1776-78** Gibbons' *Decline and Fall of the Roman Empire*. |
| **1781 to 1810** | **1383** Britain accepts American independence.<br>**1789-93** French Revolution<br>**1799** Napoleon Bonaparte takes over France.<br>**1800-15** Napoleonic wars; a series of wars between France and Europe's other great powers as Napoleon attempts to unite the whole continent through conquest.<br>**1804** Bonaparte becomes Emperor Napoleon I.<br>**1806** Napoleon reorganizes princedoms of Germany and ends the Holy Empire.<br>**1808** Beginning of the Peninsular War; England, Spain and Portugal are allies against Frace. | **1781** Immanuel Kants *Critique of Pure Reason*.<br>**1784** Death of Doctor Samuel Johnson.<br>**1785** Mozart's opera *Marriage of Figaro* first performed.<br>**1789** Robert Burns' *Poems* published with great success.<br>**1791** Mozart's *Magic Flute* first performed.<br>**1798** Wordsworth and Coleridge published *Lyrical Ballads*.<br>**1800** Beethoven's *First Symphony*.<br>**1804** *William Tell*, Schiller's final work, published.<br>**1808** Goethe's *Faust* published; Beethoven's *Fifth Symphony*. |
| **1811 to 1840** | **1814** Peninsular War ends with defeat of France. Napoleon abdicates, and is exiled to Elba.<br>**1815** Napoleon returns. After defeat at Waterloo, he is exiled to St Helena. Congress of Vienna restores many of the monarchies destroyed or deposed by Napoleon.<br>**1830** Revolution in France; Charles X, a Bourbon, replaced by Louis Philippe of Orleans.<br>**1837** Victoria becomes Queen of England.<br>**1838** Reform movement, known as Chartists after their "People's Charter", formed in England. | **1811** *Sense and Sensibility*, Jane Austen's first novel.<br>**1812** Brothers Jakob and Wilhelm Grimm produce their collected *Fairy Tales*.<br>**1817** John Constable's landscapes first exhibited.<br>**1822** First performances of Beethoven's *Missa Solemnis* and Schubert's *A Minor Symphony*.<br>**1827** Death of Beethoven.<br>**1832** Death of Goethe; *Faust II* published.<br>**1835** First major Russian novel, Gogol's *Dead Souls*.<br>**1836** Dicken's first novel, *Pickwick Papers*, appears. |
| **1841 to 1870** | **1842** Chartists riot in England.<br>**1848** The Year of Revolutions. Revolts in France, several Italian states, Vienna, Prague and Berlin. Ferdinand of Austria abdicates in favor of his nephew, Francis Joseph. Republic proclaimed in France; Bonaparte's nephew, Louis Napoleon, is elected President. In 1852, he becomes Emperor Napoleon III, as the result of a coup.<br>**1853-56** Crimean War. England, France, and Turkey allied against Russia.<br>**1854** Chartist movement disbanded.<br>**1859-61** Unification of most Italian states (not Rome). Victor Emanuel of Piedmont proclaimed King of Italy.<br>**1861-65** Civil War in U.S.A.<br>**1870** War between France and Prussia. Prussia invades, forcing Napoleon III to abdicate. Prussians besiege Paris, which proclaims a republic. Italian army enters Rome. | **1843** Richard Wagner's first opera, *The Flying Dutchman*.<br>**1845** American romantic Edgar Allan Poe publishes *Tales of Mystery* and *The Raven*. Alexandre Dumas' historical romance *Monte Cristo* appears.<br>**1847** First publication of *Jane Eyre* by Charlotte Bronte and *Wuthering Heights* by her sister, Emily.<br>**1848** Pre-Raphaelite Brotherhood founded in London. Balzac's *Comédie Humaine* completed.<br>**1850** Dicken's *David Copperfield* published. Death of Balzac and Wordsworth.<br>**1851** First edition of Melville's *Moby Dick*.<br>**1865** First publications of Lewis Carroll's *Alice in Wonderland* and Tolstoy's *War and Peace*.<br>**1866** Dostoievsky's *Crime and Punishment*.<br>**1870** Death of Charles Dickens. |
| **1871 to 1900** | **1871** Paris capitulates. William I of Prussia made Emperor (Kaiser) of Germany at Versailles.<br>**1877** Queen Victoria proclaimed Empress of India.<br>**1888** William II becomes German Kaiser; he was to remain Germany's leader until the end of the First World War.<br>**1890** Bismarck, the Prussian statesman who for 30 years presided over the unification of Germany, is dismissed.<br>**1894-5** Japan defeats China, winning Formosa.<br>**1898** Spanish-American War.<br>**1900** Boxer rebellion in China. | **1871** First Impressionist exhibition in Paris.<br>**1877** Wagner's masterwork, the four-opera cycle, *Ring des Niebelungen*, completed after 23 years.<br>**1888** Brahms' first two symphonies first performed.<br>**1890** Death of van Gogh.<br>**1895** W.B. Yeats' *Poems* and Paul Verlaine's *Confessions* published.<br>**1897** Rostand's play *Cyrano de Bergerac* opens in Paris. |

The Romantic movement in literature, music and painting, which began in the 18th century, was a reaction against the Industrial Revolution, producing geniuses like Beethoven. Individuals such as Dickens and van Gogh reacted, in turn, to the social and artistic developments of the 19th century.

| INDUSTRY AND TECHNOLOGY | RELIGION AND SOCIETY | |
|---|---|---|
| 1758 Bridgewater canal, joining the wool town of Leeds with the port of Liverpool, begun. The digging of this canal is seen by many as the beginning of the Industrial Revolution in Britain.<br>1764 James Hargreaves invents spinning jenny.<br>1779 Crompton invents spinning mule. | 1759 British Museum opens.<br>1771 Serfdom abolished in Savoy.<br>1773 Jesuits supressed by the Pope.<br>1776 Publication of Adam Smith's *Wealth of Nations* points out economic advantages of factory production. | **1750 to 1780** |
| 1775 James Watt produces the first efficient steam engine; the Age of Steam begins.<br>1785 Cartwright invents the power loom.<br>1792 Gas lighting used for the first time in England.<br>1794 Invention of cotton gin by Eli Whitney.<br>1802 Law protecting working children passed in England. First practical steamship, *Charlotte Dundas*, launched on River Clyde, Scotland. | 1781 Emperor Joseph II abolishes serfdom and introduces religious toleration in Austria.<br>1787 Association for the Abolition of the Slave Trade founded in England.<br>1789 Feudal system abolished in France.<br>1794 Slavery abolished in French colonies.<br>1807 Slave trade abolished in the British Empire. | **1781 to 1810** |
| 1811-15 The Luddites, working men who feared the loss of their livelihoods, smashed machinery all over England.<br>1814 George Stephenson tests first steam locomotive.<br>1820 First iron steamship in England.<br>1825 World's first steam locomotive railway joins northern English towns of Stockton and Darlington.<br>1826 Dutch ship makes first Atlantic crossing by steam.<br>1831 Michael Faraday discovers electromagnetism.<br>1837 Samuel Morse invents telegraph.<br>1839 Photography invented by Fox Talbot and Daguerre. | 1814 End of papal suppression of the Jesuits.<br>1819 Maximum twelve-hour working day for young workers introduced in England.<br>1829 Catholic Emancipation Act introduces religious toleration in Britain. First modern police force founded in London.<br>1833 The Oxford Movement, aimed at reintroducing ritual and mystery to the Engish Protestant church, begins.<br>1834 Emancipation of slaves in British possessions. | **1811 to 1840** |
| 1811-15 Invention of the steam hammer by James Nasmyth.<br>1851 Great Exhibition in London.<br>1854 Heinrich Goebel invents light bulbs.<br>1855 Paris World Exhibition.<br>1856 Henry Bessemer invents new, greatly improved, process for turning cast iron into steel.<br>1857 Telegraph cable laid under the Atlantic.<br>1859 Suez Canal begun. First oil well in U.S.A.<br>1862-9 Building of Central Pacific Railway across the U.S.A.<br>1863 First underground railway built in London.<br>1866 Invention of the electric dynamo by William Siemens.<br>1867 Invention of dynamite (by Dr. Alfred Nobel) and the typewriter. | 1843 First worker's cooperative society set up in Rochdale, England.<br>1848 Publication of the *Communist Manifesto* by Karl Marx and Frederick Engels. Serfdom abolished in Austria.<br>1858 Tsar Alexander II begins to emancipate the serfs.<br>1859 Publication of *Origin of the Species* by Charles Darwin, with its suggestion that man and apes have a common ancestor, causes religious upheaval.<br>1862 Final emancipation of Russian serfs.<br>1865 Slavery abolished in the U.S.A.<br>1868 Anarchist Prince Bakunin organizes the International Alliance for Social Democracy, the beginning of international socialism.<br>1870 Education Act in Britain ensures for the first time that all children get some schooling. | **1841 to 1870** |
| 1876 Alexander Graham Bell invents the telephone.<br>1877 Thomas Edison invents the phonograph.<br>1878 Invention of the repeating rifle and the microphone.<br>1883 First skyscaper (ten floors high) built in Chicago.<br>1889 Eiffel tower, then by far the tallest structure in the world, built in Paris.<br>1891-1904 Trans-Siberian Railway built across Russia.<br>1895 Marconi sends first radio message; Lumière brothers invent the cinematograph; Roëntgen discover X-rays. | 1872 Jesuits expelled from Germany.<br>1873 World-wide economic crisis.<br>1880 Roman Catholic orders expelled from France.<br>1882 California prohibits Chinese immigrants.<br>1890 International congress for protection of workers in Berlin. Anti-slavery congress in Brussels.<br>1899 International women's congress in London. | **1871 to 1900** |

# FURTHER READING

Batterberry, Ariane *The Phantheon Story of Art for Young People* (Pantheon, New York, 1975)

Blackwood, Alan *Beethoven* (Bookwright, New York, 1987)

Brownell, David *A Book of Great Composers* (Bellerphon, Santa Barbara, CA, 1978)

Collins, David R. *Tales for Hard Times: A Story about Charles Dickens* (Lerner, Minneapolis, 1990)

Cooper, Lettice *A Hand Upon the Time: A Life of Charles Dickens* (Pantheon, New York, 1966)

de Sousa, Chris *Looking at Music* (Marshall Cavendish, New York, 1989)

Greene, Carol *Ludwig van Beethoven: Musical Pioneer* (Childrens Press, Chicago, 1989)

Hunter, Nigel *Charles Dickens* (Bookwright, New York, 1989)

Jacobs, David *Beethovan* (Horizon Caravel, New York, 1970)

Johnson, Ann D. *The Value of Giving: The Story of Beethoven* (Oak Tree, San Diego, CA, 1979)

Johnson, S. *The Value of imagination: The Story of Charles Dickens* (Oak Tree, San Diego, CA, 1977)

Kennett, Frances and Terry Measham *Looking at Paintings* (Marshall Cavendish, New York, 1989)

Kyle, Elisabeth *Great Ambitions: A Story of the Early Years of Charles Dickens* (Holt, Rinehart and Winston, New York, 1966)

Lucas, Eileen *Vincent Van Gogh* (Franklin Watts, New York, 1991)

Lynton, Norbert *A History of Art: An Introduction to Paintings and Sculpture* (Warwick Press, New York, 1981)

Marri, Noemi V. *Ludwig van Beethovan* (Silver Burdett, Englewood Cliffs, NJ, 1987)

Sage, Alison *Play Beethoven* (Barron, New York, 1988)

Thames, Richard *Ludwig van Beethovan* (Franklin Watts, New York, 1991)

Venezia, Mike *Van Gogh* (Childrens Press, Chicago, 1988)

# INDEX

Fine Art Photographic Library